For my beloved Haydn G.N.

Text by Lois Rock
Illustrations copyright © 2006 Gail Newey
This edition copyright © 2006 Lion Hudson

The moral rights of the author and illustrator
have been asserted

A Lion Children's Book
an imprint of
Lion Hudson plc
Mayfield House, 256 Banbury Road,
Oxford OX2 7DH, England
www.lionhudson.com
ISBN 0 7459 4946 0

First edition 2006
10 9 8 7 6 5 4 3 2 1 0

Story text adapted from the Bible

A catalogue record for this book is available
from the British Library

Typeset in 18/26 Venetian301 BT
Printed and bound in Singapore

The Miracles of Jesus

Selected and retold by Lois Rock

Illustrated by Gail Newey

LION
CHILDREN'S

Prologue

A miracle is an event that causes people to marvel and to wonder - something so extraordinary that it seems like a blessing from God.

Two thousand years ago, the person the world knows as Jesus became known as a miracle worker.

Through all the years that he grew up in Nazareth, none of the town's people thought of him as special. He had learned the family trade and worked as a carpenter and builder. Like all young men, he had learned to read the scriptures of his people, the Jews, and was able to take his turn reading aloud from them in the synagogue.

Then he became a preacher. His message was clear: people should turn away from wrongdoing and live as friends of God. By doing so, they would be part of God's own kingdom. Their lives would be shining examples of goodness and holiness, and would help to establish peace and justice through all the world.

Many people were attracted by the things he said, and crowds gathered to listen to him. But the word spread through all the towns and villages that there was more to Jesus than wise teaching: time and again, it was rumoured, people who were sick came to him pleading for help, and he healed them. With a touch, he blessed their lives.

His close friends, the disciples, claimed that they saw him work other wonders too: the great forces of nature obeyed Jesus' command. When they did so, it was as if the world became a little more like heaven.

Through the centuries since Jesus walked this earth, the accounts of his miracles have inspired many to believe that the preacher from Nazareth was truly sent by God to bless this world. They believe he is God's son. They believe he is God's chosen king, and so they call him the Messiah, the Christ.

Contents

The wedding in Cana	6
The man in the synagogue	10
The great catch of fish	12
The hole in the roof	16
The Roman officer and his servant	19
The storm on the lake	21
The wild man of Gerasa	24
Jairus' daughter	27
Loaves and fishes	32
Walking on water	34
The ten outcasts	37
The man born blind	40
Lazarus	44
Epilogue	48

The wedding in Cana

In the towns and villages of Galilee, a wedding was always a time of feasting and merriment. People would be invited from far and wide, and it was very important for the host to be generous in providing for the guests.

One day, there was a wedding in a place called Cana. Jesus' mother was invited, and so was Jesus himself, along with his band of disciples. The bride and groom sat smiling under a canopy of greenery and flowers. Around them a multitude of guests were eating and drinking, singing and dancing.

In the middle of the festivity, Jesus'
mother came hurrying to find her son.
She looked anxious as she whispered,
'They have no wine left.' Then she looked
at Jesus as if hoping for something.

'You mustn't tell me what to do,'
replied Jesus. 'My time has not yet come.'

Jesus' mother bustled away to speak
with the servants. 'If my son tells you to
do anything, you must be sure to do it,' she said firmly. Then she glanced
back at her son before returning to talk to her friends and neighbours.

At a table near Jesus, some young men held a large jug upside down.
'Empty again,' they laughed. 'How did we manage to get through that lot?
More importantly, where can we fetch more wine? Who's in charge of this
event - he should know!'

While one of their number set off with the empty jug, Jesus went straight
over to the servants. 'These big jars here,' he said, pointing to six stone jars
that were used to store water for washing. 'I want you to fill them with
water, all of them.'

It was hard work. The jars were huge, and the servants had to bring pitcher after pitcher from the well before they managed to fill each one to the brim with water.

'Now draw off a little water and take it to the man in charge of the feast,' said Jesus.

A servant obeyed at once, and the man in charge of the feast took a sip.

'Mmm,' he said. 'Very good. Very good indeed,' He beckoned to the bridegroom so he could speak to him.

'I'm impressed,' he said. 'The usual thing to do at a wedding is to serve the best wine first and then bring out the cheaper stuff when people have already had plenty to drink. You have kept the best till now.'

This was the first miracle Jesus performed. It gave his disciples a glimpse of his power.

From John 2:1-12

The man in the synagogue

Jesus was a Jew and he had been brought up in the traditions of his people.

It was the custom for every Jewish community to meet in their synagogue once a week, on the Sabbath day of rest. There they would listen as a short piece of scripture was read aloud and explained. Jesus himself was becoming well known as someone who could talk wisely about the Jewish faith.

One day, not long after Jesus had moved from his home in Nazareth to Capernaum, he was invited to teach in the synagogue. There was a man there who could not stop himself from shouting and screaming. Some power that was greater than him had him in its grip.

'What do you want with us, Jesus of Nazareth?' he cried. 'Are you here to destroy us? I know who you are: you are God's holy messenger.'

Jesus spoke to the evil thing that was destroying the man. 'Be quiet. Come out of that man,' he said.

The man fell to the ground with an ugly scream. Then, when he sat up, he found himself in the middle of the synagogue with everyone looking at him. Suddenly, he wanted to take his proper place alongside his relatives.

'Sorry,' he murmured. Quickly and quietly, he went and found a seat.

'Jesus has healed him,' people began to whisper. 'What is so special about the words he utters? What kind of power does he command?'

They gossiped the news of this miracle far and wide. When the sun set, marking the end of the Sabbath, everyone who had friends or relatives who were unwell brought them to Jesus and pleaded for him to heal them. With just a touch of his hands he healed them all.

From Luke 4:31-36 and 40

The great catch of fish

Jesus became well known as a teacher and miracle worker. Everywhere he went, crowds were eager to see him.

One day, he began preaching on the shore of Lake Galilee.

The gathering crowd pressed closer and closer: no one wanted to miss a word he said.

Jesus was concerned that people who wanted to see him and hear him could not do so. He looked around, wondering what he could do. There, a little further along the beach, were two fishing boats. His friend and disciple, Simon, was sitting nearby with some other fishermen and they were all mending their nets.

Jesus walked over to Simon's boat. 'Can you push this further out into the lake for me?' he called to his friend. 'Of course,' said Simon. 'Come on, lads, let's slide this thing back into the lake.'

Jesus climbed aboard just as the boat hit the water. He found a place to perch where everyone could see him, and then he began talking to the crowd once more.

When he had finished, he called to Simon. 'Push the boat out further now. You and the others can let your nets down for a catch.'

'Master,' said Simon. 'We were fishing all night and caught nothing.'

Jesus simply smiled.

'Oh, we can try if you like,' said Simon. 'We'll soon find out if you know more about fishing than I do.'

He and his friends James and John took the two boats out and let their nets down. In no time, the nets were heavy with a huge catch of fish. 'Over here, over here,' called Simon, beckoning to the men in the other boat. 'You're going to have to come over here if we're going to haul this lot on board.'

They puffed and groaned with the effort of heaving such a huge amount
of fish.

'Careful!' shouted one of the fishermen. 'This is going to sink the lot of us.'

Once they were safe, Simon turned to Jesus and fell on his knees. 'Listen,' he
said. 'I really respect you as a teacher,' he said, 'but… you're too good for me.
I'm just an ordinary man with loads of faults. I think you should go about
your work without my help from now on.'

'Don't be afraid,' replied Jesus. 'From now on, you are going to be fishing
for God, gathering people into God's kingdom.'

Something in Jesus' manner persuaded them all. The fishermen pulled their
boats onto the beach. They left everything they had and followed Jesus.

from Luke 5:1-11

The hole in the roof

News of Jesus' teaching was reaching further and further. The religious leaders had to take notice of it: it was clear that the crowds adored him. They, however, were concerned that some of what he said was not in keeping with the Law as they understood it.

A large number of them arranged to meet with him. They came not only from Galilee but also from distant Judea and the great city of Jerusalem. Soon the house where they were meeting was full, and still the ordinary people kept on coming in the hope of seeing Jesus.

A group of men came along, carrying a man on his sleeping mat as if it were a stretcher.

'This is hopeless,' they sighed, when they saw the crowds. 'We're all sure that Jesus could cure you so you could walk; but we're not going to get near him at this rate.'

They wandered round the house, but every doorway was crammed with people. 'Let's rest here,' said one. 'We can sit on the steps here and think.'

The outdoor steps led onto the flat roof, which was used for storing things. 'Hey, I've an idea,' said another. 'Let's go up here. This is my plan…'

Together they carried their friend onto the roof and the man explained what

he had in mind. Laughing at their own boldness, they scraped away the roof covering: first the tiles, then the plaster and the network of branches and twigs that held it together. They waved merrily down to the sea of puzzled faces, and then let their friend down on ropes, right in front of Jesus.

'Help him,' called the men. 'We know you can heal anyone!'

'Do you really believe that?' asked Jesus.

'Of course!' they cried. 'You've got miraculous powers, haven't you?'

Jesus turned to the man on the bed. 'Your sins are forgiven, my friend,' he said.

At that, the religious leaders began to look at one another uneasily.

Some began to murmur. 'Did you hear that? How dare this self-taught preacher forgive sins? Only God can do that.'

'It's blasphemy,' whispered an older man. 'That's about the worse crime against our law!'

Jesus looked up. 'What is easier to say?' he asked. ' "Your sins are forgiven" or "Pick up your bed and walk"? The first might be empty words. The second will show you whether or not I have authority from God to forgive.'

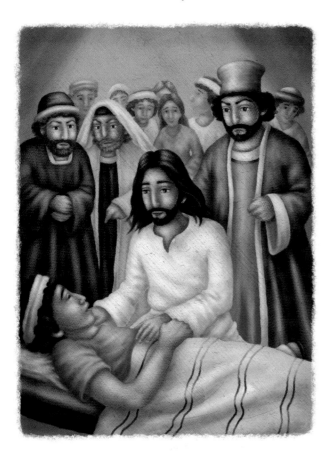

He turned back to the man at his feet.

'I'm telling you to get up, pick up your bed, and go home.'

The man pushed himself to sitting. Then he scrambled to his feet.

'Bless you!' he cried. 'Praise God, I can walk!'

The crowds watched him dancing out of the house. They were utterly amazed.

From Luke 5:17-25

The Roman officer and his servant

The land where Jesus lived was part of the Roman empire. The Jewish people, like so many others in the empire, had to accept that Roman soldiers policed them. They nevertheless treated the foreign troops as outsiders.

One Roman officer lived in Capernaum. He had great respect for the Jewish faith, and in return he had won the respect of local people. One day, when his household was in crisis, he called upon the elders of the community to help him.

'One of my most valuable servants is desperately ill,' he explained to them. 'Now, I have heard of this preacher, Jesus, who is reputed to have healed many people. Can you go to him and ask him to help? I cannot think of any other solution.'

The elders took the message to Jesus, and Jesus agreed to go with them back to the officer's house.

While they were on their way, some messengers arrived to speak to him.

'The officer says this: please don't trouble yourself to come to my house. I am not worthy to receive you, nor am I worthy to come to you myself. Just give the order for my servant to be well. I myself accept the authority of senior officers, and I have authority over my soldiers. If I tell someone to do something, he does it.'

Jesus looked round and spoke to the crowd who were following him. 'I haven't found anyone with faith like this even among my own people.'

He nodded towards the messengers and they hurried back to the officer's house.

They arrived to discover that the servant was well again.

From Luke 7:1-10

The storm on the lake

Jesus the teacher was eager to spread his message: he wanted everyone to know about God's love and forgiveness.

As he travelled around the region of Galilee, he and his disciples often used a boat to sail across the lake. Several of his disciples were fishermen, and they were well used to handling their craft in all weathers.

So it was that one evening, after a busy day speaking to the crowds, Jesus got on the boat and fell fast asleep, leaving his disciples to take care of the sailing. The water lapped gently against the sides and a gentle breeze filled the sail.

In the night, without warning, a strong wind came howling down from the hills. It ripped at the sail and whipped the water into waves.

'Get the sail down,' shrieked one of the fishermen. 'Grab the bailer. We're taking on water.'

The men battled to bring the boat to safety, but the storm grew more and more violent.

'Jesus!' they shouted. Someone went to shake him by the shoulder. 'Wake up! We're about to die.'

Jesus sat up slowly and blinked. 'What's the matter?' he asked in puzzled tones.

'We're at risk of drowning!' came the shrieked reply. 'Don't you care?'

Jesus stood up and looked around him. Then he spoke. 'Listen to me, you howling wind,' he said, 'be quiet.'

A wave seized the boat and tipped it at a dizzying angle. Jesus grabbed the side. 'You waves, you must listen too. Lie down.'

The boat rocked for a moment, and then was still. The waves rippled away. The wind whispered to nothing.

'There,' said Jesus to the disciples. 'Where is your faith?'

The men glanced at one another and then looked down. They turned back to their tasks. Jesus lay down.

'Is he asleep again?' asked one.

'I think so,' came the reply. 'What happened there?'

'Who is he,' added a third, 'that even the winds and waves obey him?'

From Luke 8:22-25

The wild man of Gerasa

Jesus and his disciples sailed to the region of Gerasa, on the far side of the lake. As Jesus stepped out of the boat, a wild-looking man came shrieking down to meet him. He was completely naked, and his bare skin was sun-scorched and scarred. Around his wrists and ankles were iron bands from which a few links of chain clattered uselessly - the remnants of shackles that had been broken by sheer brute strength.

Jesus spoke quietly: 'Listen to me, you evil powers that are driving that man crazy. Leave him alone.'

The man uttered an unearthly howl and threw himself at Jesus' feet. 'Jesus, son of the Most High God, what do you want? I beg you, don't punish me.'

'What is your name?' asked Jesus.

'I'm home to a mob of demons, I can't name them all!' laughed the man bitterly. 'Just call me Mob.'

'In that case, I want the entire Mob to listen to me. Leave that man - '

'No! No! No!' howled the man. 'The demons are at home in me. They'll die if you send them away. At least give them a new home... lizards, locusts, even those pigs over there.'

He clung on to Jesus' feet, whimpering like a frightened child.

Jesus looked up to where a herd of pigs were rooting around on a steep hillside.

'Then go to the pigs,' he said.

The man gave a shriek and collapsed. The pigs began to run - the whole herd began galloping wildly down the hillside and tumbled off the edge of the cliff into the lake.

The men in charge of the pigs stood open-mouthed. They turned to look at one another and then they fled.

Soon they had told their story in the nearby town. Many people came hurrying out, to see for themselves what had happened and who it was who had caused it.

They found Jesus and the wild man talking quietly together. 'Something amazing has happened,' they whispered. 'Look - they've found clean clothes for him and he's actually wearing them. He's talking and listening like a man in his right mind.'

'It's like we told you,' explained one of the men. 'Jesus just spoke a few words, and a miracle happened.'

'I can't explain it and I don't like it,' growled an older man. 'I want that preacher out of here - let him go back to his own town.'

He had the crowd on his side. They surged forward threateningly. 'Go,' they shouted to Jesus. 'Troublemaker. If that's your boat, get on it. Go.'

'Let me come with you,' said the man who had been healed.

'I want you to stay,' said Jesus. 'Go back home and tell everyone what God has done for you.'

From Luke 8:26-39

Jairus' daughter

Jesus and his disciples were sailing back to their own side of the lake. Down by the shore, a huge crowd was gathering, eager to see Jesus again.

Among the throng was a man named Jairus. He was an official at the local synagogue, and perhaps it was out of respect for his position that people let him through to the front.

Jairus threw himself to the ground at Jesus' feet.

'Please,' he begged, 'come to my house. My daughter is dying - she is only twelve years old. Perhaps you can heal her before it is too late.'

Jesus agreed at once, and Jairus led the way.

On every side the crowd pushed and surged - now this way, now the other. People were calling Jesus' name. Hands were reaching out to touch him. All at once, Jesus stopped and looked around.

'Who touched me?' he said. His expression was stern, almost fierce. Everyone stepped back.

'It wasn't me, wasn't me.' Everyone mumbled and looked away.

'Come on, Master,' said Peter. 'Look at the number of people. It could have been anyone who touched you - whatever they did, it was surely an accident.'

'No,' said Jesus. 'Someone touched me deliberately and I felt power go out of me.'

As he gazed round, a woman whose face was lined with sorrow began to tremble. Shakily, she stepped closer and fell to her knees.

'It was me,' she confessed. 'I've had a problem for years - bleeding and bleeding, and no one able to help me. I just thought... maybe... and then you'd passed me by and I just touched the edge of your cloak... and you're right. I'm healed, aren't I? Already I feel so well.'

Jesus smiled. 'Your faith has made you well,' he said. 'Go in peace.'

Just at that moment, a messenger arrived from Jairus' house.

'I'm sorry,' he whispered to the father. 'Your daughter... she died just a little while ago. Come back to the house. You don't need to bother the Teacher any longer.'

Jesus took Jairus' arm. 'Come,' he said. 'Don't be afraid; just believe, and your daughter will be well.' As they approached the house, they heard the sound of women wailing: already the mourners had gathered, and they were noisy in their grief.

'Don't cry,' said Jesus. 'The girl isn't dead; she's only sleeping.'

'How dare you say that?' retorted one of the women, angrily.

'You think you're so special, don't

you,' sneered another. 'When did you last wash a body for a funeral?'

'You come to a house where tragedy has struck and you talk nonsense. Don't you understand how hurtful that can be? You arrogant young upstart!'

The women behind all joined in the jeering.

'Let's go inside,' said Jesus to Jairus. 'Peter, John and James, you can come too.'

The mother led the men to the room where her daughter lay on the bed. Her body was still and cold.

Jesus walked up to her. He took her hand. 'Come, little girl, get up,' he said.

The girl turned her head and opened her eyes. Her mother rushed to hug her, and sat with her, laughing and crying at the same time. Jairus clutched Jesus' hand in thanks and then went to wrap his arms round both of them.

'I'm really hungry,' said the little girl.

'I'll go now,' whispered Jesus. 'You need to give your daughter something to eat. There's just one thing I'd like to ask of you... don't tell anyone about what happened.'

From Luke 8:40-56

Loaves and fishes

Sometimes, it seemed to Jesus' disciples that they could never escape the crowds.

'We sailed over here to Bethsaida for some peace and quiet,' they groaned. 'Just look along the road... there are hundreds of people coming - thousands, even. How did they find out where we were heading? How did they get around the lake so quickly?'

'We should be pleased to see them,' replied Jesus. 'I certainly am. Come on - this is an opportunity to spread the news about God's kingdom.'

He stood up and preached to the people, and they hung on his every word. As the sun began to sink towards the horizon, the disciples decided it was time for him to stop.

'You've got to send the people away now,' they explained. 'They're all too far from where they've come from to go home. They must be getting hungry and tired.'

'Then give them something to eat,' replied Jesus.

The twelve looked at him, their expression one of disbelief. 'That would cost a fortune!' they exclaimed. 'A fortune that we don't have.'

'Well then, find out what people have got to share,' said Jesus.

The disciples shrugged and began making enquiries, but it wasn't long before they trooped back to Jesus, Andrew leading the way. 'Here's a boy who's brought some food,' he explained. 'He's happy to let you use it all. Do you want to know the size of his little feast? It's five loaves of bread and two small fish.'

'Good,' said Jesus, seeming quite untroubled. 'Now I want you to organize everyone so they are in groups of about fifty. After that, I'll give you the food.'

When the people were sitting down and ready, Jesus took the loaves and fishes and said a prayer of thanks to God. He broke the food into pieces and gave some to each disciple. They took what they had to the people, one group after another.

Somehow, there was always more. Everyone ate all they wanted. When they had all finished, the disciples gathered up the scraps, and these alone filled twelve baskets.

From Luke 9:10-17

Walking on water

After Jesus had fed a great crowd of people with just five loaves and two fish, he sent the people away. Then he turned to his disciples.

'I want you to sail the boat to the other side of the lake. I'm going to stay here and pray. I'll meet up with you later.'

The men set out in the little boat. 'We won't be sailing as such,' they groaned. 'The wind is dead against us. We'll have to take turns at the oars. Off we go.'

They struggled to make progress and groaned with the effort of rowing against the headwind. As the night wore on, they found themselves in the middle of the lake. They had long ceased making progress: they were simply being tossed by the waves.

It was then that Jesus came back down to the shore and saw them, the boat a dark shape against the glimmering water.

He began walking to catch up with them... not by the path around the lake, but straight across the water. The eastern edge of the sky was paling with the dawn when the disciples glimpsed a shadowy figure among the waves.

The men at the oars stopped rowing and gazed in fear. 'Is it a ghost?' they asked one another. 'Surely not? But... what else could it be?'

'Who's that?' they shrieked. 'What do you want?'

'Don't be afraid,' came the cheerful reply. 'It's me - Jesus.'

'Jesus!' whispered Peter to himself. 'Really?' Then he called out. 'If it's really you, then order me to come out on the water and walk to you.'

'Yes, come,' replied Jesus, waving cheerfully.

'Here I go lads,' muttered Peter, as he climbed over the side of the boat.

His feet touched the water. He wasn't sinking. Hesitantly, he let go of the side of the boat and began walking, holding his arms out sideways, as if for balance. He looked up towards Jesus. 'Help! There's a huge wave,' he began... but already the curling water had knocked him over.

'Help!' he screamed. 'I'm sinking!'

At once Jesus reached out and grabbed him. 'What happened to your faith?' he said. 'Why did you doubt that you could do it? Come on, into the boat.'

As soon as Jesus had climbed into the boat, the wind died down.

The disciples bowed their heads in awe. 'That was amazing,' they whispered. 'Truly, you must be the Son of God.'

From Matthew 14:22-32

The ten outcasts

Jesus and his disciples were travelling to Jerusalem. They had chosen the road that skirted the border between his own region of Galilee and another called Samaria. Hundreds of years before, the people of Samaria had developed their own religious traditions. The differences between theirs and those of the Jewish people had given rise to mistrust and even hatred.

Jesus was going by a village when he saw a group of men sitting by the side of the road. They saw him too, and they stood up as if to go.

'Look!' murmured one. 'It's that Jesus... the one who's supposed to be able to heal people.'

'Jesus!' shouted another. 'Master! Have pity on us.'

Then they all began calling out. 'Help us! You know what it is we're suffering from. We're not even allowed home to our villages round here, everyone's so afraid of us.'

Jesus looked at them. Their disfigured skin clearly showed that they had the dreaded skin disease that made them outcasts. He nodded. 'I've heard you,' he said. 'Now go to the priests and ask them to declare you officially well. Only then will you be allowed to come and go as you please.'

He turned to continue his journey.

'Well,' said the men to each other. 'What are we to make of that? Shall we go to the priest anyway?'

'I don't know what the priest will say when we turn up looking like this,' said one.

'Actually, you're looking better than you have been,' came the reply. 'Just a moment - you know, your face looks completely healthy.'

The speaker glanced down at his own hands. 'Look - I'm better too,' he said. 'Hey, you lot - look at yourselves.'

Every one of them had clear, smooth skin again. The disease and its terrible scarring had vanished.

'Come on!' shouted one. 'We've no time to lose!'

Nine of them raced away. The tenth stood still for a moment, then turned in the direction Jesus had taken. As soon as he caught a glimpse of him, he began to shout.

'Jesus! Wait! Praise the Lord! You've healed me!' he cried.

Jesus looked back. The man flung himself at Jesus' feet. 'Thank you! Thank God!' he almost sobbed.

'Only you?' asked Jesus. 'There were ten of you healed. Where are the other nine?'

He looked at his disciples. 'This man is a Samaritan, yet only he has come back to thank God,' he told them.

He turned back to the man. 'Get up and go on your way. Your faith has made you well.'

From Luke 17:11-19

The man born blind

One day as Jesus was walking along, he and his disciples passed a beggar by the side of the road.

'Look at him,' said the disciples. 'He's been blind since the day he was born. Whose fault is that, Jesus? Did he do something wrong - or is it his parents who are at fault?'

'Neither,' replied Jesus. 'He is blind so that God's power can be seen at work in him. While I am here in the world, I am the light for the world.'

Jesus stopped. He spat on the ground and mixed the dirt to make some mud. 'I'm going to put this mud on your eyes,' he explained to the blind man. 'It's like a poultice a doctor would apply. After that, I want you to go to the pool of Siloam and wash it off.'

The man went. As he wiped his eyes clean he gasped in astonishment. 'This is what it means to see!' he whispered. He stood up. 'I can see!' he cried. 'I can see!'

Some of his neighbours were standing nearby. 'Is that who it looks like? Isn't that the man who used to sit and beg?'

'It is him, you know. I've watched him grow up... he's always been blind.'

'It can't be him then. Everyone said his blindness could never be cured.'

The man overheard the gossiping. 'Yes, I'm the person you think. The man called Jesus just healed me. It's amazing, isn't it? Such a simple thing he did...'

The people took the man to see the religious leaders, who were Pharisees. They listened to the story, grim faced. 'Tell us again what happened,' they said.

'Jesus put some mud on my eyes; I washed my face - now I can see,' replied

the man. 'He's a prophet, that Jesus.'

The Pharisees shook their heads. 'He's no prophet! He's done something on the Sabbath that can only count as work, and that's against God's laws. He can't possibly have God's power to heal.'

'Though there is a small problem with our reasoning,' countered one. 'The man has been cured.'

'Not necessarily,' replied another. 'Maybe he faked his blindness. I wonder what his parents would say.'

The man's parents were sent for. They were laughing and crying at once as they hugged their grown-up son. 'He was blind as a baby,' sobbed the mother. 'Now he can see. Oh, I've dreamed of this happening.'

'Your son says that Jesus healed him... that so-called prophet whom some people are calling the Messiah.'

'Oh, you'll have to ask him about that,' said the father, suddenly getting serious. 'He's old enough to make up his mind about that sort of thing. We don't want to get mixed up in any religious arguments, thank you.'

The Pharisees called the man back. 'You must promise before God to tell the truth. We know that the man who cured you is a sinner.'

The man shrugged, 'I don't know if he's a sinner or not,' he said. 'One thing I do know: I was blind and now I see.'

His remark sparked off a bitter argument. In the end, the Pharisees told the man he could no longer be part of their synagogue meetings. When Jesus heard about all of this, he went and found the man.

'Do you believe in the Son of Man?' he asked.

'Tell me who he is,' replied the man, 'so I can believe in him.'

Jesus said to him, 'You have already seen him, and he is the one who is talking with you now.'

'I believe, Lord!' the man said, and he knelt down before Jesus.

From John 9:1-38

Lazarus

Among Jesus' close friends were a man named Lazarus and his sisters, Martha and Mary.

One day, the sisters sent Jesus a message: 'Lord, your dear friend is ill.'

'Oh,' sighed Jesus. 'This is bad news. However, it's not going to end with the death of Lazarus. It's going to be something that brings glory to God and the Son of God.'

He looked at his disciples. 'We shall stay here for two more days,' he said. 'Then we will go.'

'Is that a good idea?' asked the disciples. 'The people down there in Bethany got a bit worked up last time you were there - they were planning to stone you to death, remember?'

'They need to see things more clearly,' explained Jesus. 'When I go and wake Lazarus, they will.'

'Why bother?' asked the disciples. 'If he's sleeping, he'll wake up by himself.'

'I was putting it gently,' explained Jesus. 'He's dead. I want people to believe in me when they see what I can do.'

The disciple called Thomas shrugged. 'I suppose we agreed to follow you.

If we die together down in Bethany, we die together.'

They finally arrived to find that Lazarus had been buried four days earlier. Friends and relatives had arrived from nearby Jerusalem to mourn. Mary was weeping in the house. Martha went out to greet Jesus.

'You've come,' she sobbed, 'but too late. If only you'd been here, my brother would not have died. But even so, God will give you whatever you ask - I can believe that, can't I?' She trailed off in tears.

'Your brother will rise to life,' said Jesus.

'Yes, on the last day he will,' she agreed sadly.

'Martha,' said Jesus. 'I am the resurrection and the life. Those who believe in me will live, even though they die; and all those who live and believe in me will never die. Do you believe this?'

Martha nodded as bravely as she could. 'Yes, Lord!' she answered. 'I do believe that you are the Messiah, the Son of God, who was to come into the world.'

She hurried off to tell Mary of Jesus' arrival, and Mary came out of the house sobbing. 'If only you'd been here,' she told him, almost angrily, 'my brother wouldn't have died.' All around her the mourners broke out weeping and wailing.

'Come on,' said Jesus. 'Show me where he's buried.'

The people led him to a cave. A huge stone had been rolled over the entrance. It seemed like a symbol of the awful finality of death. Jesus wept. The

mourners nudged one another. 'See, he really was fond of Lazarus. It's not his fault the young man died.'

'He's worked so many other miracles, though. Couldn't he have kept Lazarus from dying?'

Jesus walked towards the tomb. 'Please roll back this stone door,' he said.

'No!' cried Martha. 'The body has been there four days. It will smell...'

'Trust me,' said Jesus.

Strong people rolled back the door. Jesus looked up to heaven and said a prayer:

'I thank you, Father, that you listen to me. I know that you always listen to me, but I say this for the sake of the people here, so that they will believe that you sent me.'

Then he called out in a loud voice: 'Lazarus, come out.'

For a moment, nothing happened. Then a figure emerged from the blackness within.

It was Lazarus, and he was tugging at the linen bandages in which he had been wrapped for his burial.

'Come on, help untie him,' said Jesus, 'and let him begin life again.'

From John 11:1-44

Epilogue

Jesus' preaching about God's kingdom came to a sudden end. The religious leaders plotted his death. It was on a Friday that they finally had him crucified. Jesus' friends had little time to lay his body in a tomb before the Sabbath day of rest.

Early on the Sunday morning, a small group of women went back to the tomb, hoping simply to be able to wrap the body according to the proper funeral traditions.

They found the tomb open and the body gone. Yet, within minutes, they came rushing back to find the other disciples with amazing news: angels had told them that God had raised Jesus to life.

Over the next few weeks, the despair of Jesus' friends and followers turned to joy. They said that they had seen Jesus alive and spoken with him. He had told them that he wanted them to go on spreading the news about God's kingdom.

They proclaimed that the resurrection was the greatest miracle of all: a sign from God that death is not the end, and that those who follow Jesus will find their everlasting home in God's heaven.